The Dairy Group

by Helen Frost

Consulting Editor: Gail Saunders-Smith, Ph.D.

Consultant: Linda Hathaway
Health Educator
McMillen Center for Health Education

Pebble Books

an imprint of Capstone Press
Mankato, Minnesota

Pebble Books are published by Capstone Press
151 Good Counsel Drive, P.O. Box 669, Mankato, Minnesota 56002
http://www.capstone-press.com

2 3 4 5 6 05 04 03 02

Library of Congress Cataloging-in-Publication Data
Frost, Helen, 1949–
    The dairy group/by Helen Frost.
    p. cm.—(The food guide pyramid)
    Includes bibliographical references and index.
    Summary: Simple text and photographs present the foods that are part of the
dairy group and their nutritional importance.
    ISBN 0-7368-0540-0 (hardcover)
    ISBN 0-7368-4890-8 (paperback)
    1. Nutrition—Juvenile literature. 2. Dairy products—Juvenile literature.
[1. Dairy products. 2. Nutrition.] I. Title. II. Series.
TX355.F765 2000
613.2—dc21   99-047740

Note to Parents and Teachers

The Food Guide Pyramid series supports national science standards
related to physical health and nutrition. This book describes and
illustrates the dairy group. The photographs support early readers
in understanding the text. The repetition of words and phrases
helps early readers learn new words. This book also introduces
early readers to subject-specific vocabulary words, which are
defined in the Words to Know section. Early readers may need
assistance to read some words and to use the Table of Contents,
Words to Know, Read More, Internet Sites, and Index/Word List
sections of the book.

Table of Contents

The food guide pyramid shows the foods you need to stay healthy. The dairy group is near the top of the food guide pyramid.

Dairy foods are
made from milk.

You can choose foods
in the dairy group
that are low in fat.

Milk is in
the dairy group.

Cheese is in
the dairy group.

Yogurt is in
the dairy group.

Pudding is in
the dairy group.

Cottage cheese is in the dairy group.

You need two to three servings from the dairy group every day. Foods in the dairy group make your teeth and bones strong.

Words to Know

dairy foods—foods that are made from milk

fat—an oily substance found in the bodies of animals and some plants; you need only a small amount of fat.

food guide pyramid—a triangle split into six areas to show the different foods people need; a pyramid is big at the bottom and small at the top; people need more food from the bottom of the food guide pyramid than from the top.

serving—a helping of food or drink; one serving from the dairy group is two ounces (55 grams) of cheese or one cup (250 ml) of milk or yogurt.

Read More

Bryant-Mole, Karen. *Food.* Picture This! Crystal Lake, Ill.: Rigby, 1997.

Frost, Helen. *Eating Right.* The Food Guide Pyramid. Mankato, Minn.: Pebble Books, 2000.

Kalbacken, Joan. *The Food Pyramid.* A True Book. New York: Children's Press, 1998.

Powell, Jillian. *Milk.* Everyone Eats. Austin, Texas: Raintree Steck-Vaughn, 1997.

Internet Sites

Got Milk?: Better Bones
http://www.got-milk.com/bones.html

Nutrition & the Food Pyramid
http://www2.lhric.org/pocantico/nutrition/nutrition.html

The Story of Milk
http://www.moomilk.com/tour.htm

Index/Word List

Word Count: 97
Early-Intervention Level: 13

Editorial Credits

Mari C. Schuh, editor; Heather Kindseth, cover designer; Sara A. Sinnard, illustrator; Kia Bielke, illustrator; Kimberly Danger, photo researcher

Photo Credits

David F. Clobes, 1, 8
Gregg R. Andersen, cover
Kim Stanton, 12
Matt Swinden, 18
Photri-Microstock, 10
Spectrum Photographics/David F. Clobes Stock Photography, 16
Unicorn Stock Photos/Wayne Floyd, 6; Robin Rudd, 14
Uniphoto/John Coletti, 20